Series MB3 no. 20

Congenital Anomaly Statistics Notifications

A statistical review of notifications of congenital anomalies received as part of the England and Wales National Congenital Anomaly System, 2005

© Crown copyright 2006
Published with the permission of the Controller of Her Majesty's Stationery Office (HMSO)

ISBN (10) 1-85774-640-6
ISBN (13) 978-1-85774-640-2
ISSN 1460-3934

You may re-use this publication (excluding logos) free of charge in any format for research, private study or internal circulation within an organisation. You must re-use it accurately and not use it in a misleading context. The material must be acknowledged as Crown copyright and you must give the title of the source publication. Where we have identified any third party copyright material you will need to obtain permission from the copyright holders concerned.

This publication is also available at the National Statistics website: www.statistics.gov.uk

For any other use of this material please apply for a Click-Use Licence for core material at www.opsi.gov.uk/click-use/system/online/pLogin.asp or by writing to:
Office of Public Sector Information
Information Policy Team
St Clements House
2–16 Colegate
Norwich NR3 1BQ
Fax: 01603 723000
E-mail: hmsolicensing@cabinet-office.x.gsi.gov.uk

Contact points
For enquiries about this publication, contact
Vital Statistics Output Branch
Tel: 01329 813758
E-mail: vsob@ons.gsi.gov.uk

For general enquiries, contact the National Statistics Customer Contact Centre on: 0845 601 3034
(minicom: 01633 812399)
E-mail: info@statistics.gsi.gov.uk
Fax: 01633 652747
Post: Room 1015, Government Buildings,
Cardiff Road, Newport NP10 8XG

You can also find National Statistics on the Internet at:
www.statistics.gov.uk

About the Office for National Statistics
The Office for National Statistics (ONS) is the government agency responsible for compiling, analysing and disseminating many of the United Kingdom's economic, social and demographic statistics, including the retail prices index, trade figures and labour market data, as well as the periodic census of the population and health statistics. It is also the agency that administers the statutory registration of births, marriages and deaths in England and Wales. The Director of ONS is also the National Statistician and the Registrar General for England and Wales.

A National Statistics publication
National Statistics are produced to high professional standards set out in the National Statistics Code of Practice. They undergo regular quality assurance reviews to ensure that they meet customer needs. They are produced free from any political influence.

Contents

			Page
Introduction			v
General notes			vii
Table 1	Summary table – Congenital anomaly notifications, Abortion notifications, 2005	England and Wales Areas covered by local registers. Areas not covered by local registers	1
Table 2a	Live and stillborn babies notified - numbers: sex by condition, 2005	England and Wales	2
Table 2b	Live and stillborn babies notified - rates per 10,000 live/stillbirths: sex by condition, 2005	England and Wales	3
Table 3	All babies notified - numbers: number of reported anomalies, 2005	England and Wales	4
Table 4a	Live and stillborn babies notified - numbers: multiplicity by condition, 2005	England and Wales	5
Table 4b	Live and stillborn babies notified - rates per 10,000 live/stillbirths: multiplicity by condition, 2005	England and Wales	5
Table 5a	Total (live and still) births, all babies notified - numbers: condition by area of usual residence of mother, 2005	England and Wales	6
Table 5b	All babies notified - rates per 10,000 total births: condition by area of usual residence of mother, 2005	England and Wales	8
Table 6a	All babies notified - numbers: month of birth by condition, 2005	England and Wales	10
Table 6b	All babies notified - rates per 10,000 total births: month of birth by condition, 2005	England and Wales	10
Table 7a	Live and stillborn babies notified - numbers: birthweight by condition, 2005	England and Wales	12
Table 7b	Live and stillborn babies notified - rates per 10,000 live/stillbirths: birthweight by condition, 2005	England and Wales	13
Table 8a	All babies notified - numbers: age of mother by condition, 2005	England and Wales	14
Table 8b	All babies notified - rates per 10,000 total births: age of mother by condition, 2005	England and Wales	14
Table 8c	All babies - numbers: age of mother by condition, 2005	Areas covered by local registers	15
Table 8d	All babies - rates per 10,000 total births: age of mother by condition, 2005	Areas covered by local registers	15

			Page
Table 8e	All babies - numbers: age of mother by condition, 2005	Areas not covered by local registers	16
Table 8f	All babies - rates per 10,000 total births: age of mother by condition, 2005	Areas not coverd by local registers	16
Table 9	Strategic Health Authorities in England, and Wales which have shown an increase of numbers of a particular anomaly compared with the average notification for that area and anomaly during a previous period, 2005	England and Wales	17
Table 10	All babies notified compared with the numbers published in the 2004 annual reference volume and Health Statistics Quarterly 29, 1995-2005	England and Wales	19
Appendix A	List of conditions for exclusion		20
Appendix B	Example of congenital anomalies notifications form (SD56)		21
Appendix C	List of ICD10 codes included within anomaly groups		22
Appendix D	ONS Monitoring groups and ICD10 equivalent codes		23
Appendix E	Summary table - Congenital anomaly notifications, Abortion notifications, Stillbirths, Neonatal deaths, 2004	England and Wales	24

Introduction

The monitoring scheme

This is the twentieth in a series of annual reference volumes and presents information collected through the National Congenital Anomaly System (NCAS) for 2005.

Since 1964 the Office for National Statistics (ONS) has run a monitoring system for congenital anomalies in England and Wales. This notification system was initiated following the thalidomide epidemic in order to quickly detect any similar hazard. The primary purpose of this system is to detect changes in the frequency of reporting any particular anomaly or group of anomalies rather than trying to estimate the prevalence at birth. From 1st January 1995 anomalies detected at any age can be reported to the NCAS.

The congenital anomaly notification system, which is voluntary at all stages, is usually linked to the statutory system of birth notification to local health authorities which has existed since 1926. The local health authorities extract from the birth notifications details of babies born with anomalies. This information is commonly supplemented with details obtained from midwives, hospitals, doctors and health visitors.

Prior to 1990 all anomalies, however minor, were reportable to ONS. In January 1990 an exclusion list was introduced (a copy of the exclusion list is at **Appendix A**). This list describes the minor anomalies which should no longer be notified to ONS.

Information about babies with congenital anomalies is forwarded to ONS on a standard form (a copy of the reporting form used for the period covered by this volume is at **Appendix B**). Following the restructuring of the National Health Service in 1974 the information was passed to ONS by the area health authorities (AHAs) and their respective area Medical Officers. When AHAs were abolished in March 1982 the work was taken over by the district health authorities (DHAs) and their district Medical Officers.

Since the reforms following the NHS and Community Care Act 1990, the notification forms have been completed by NHS Trusts, which receive birth notifications on behalf of the Health Authority.

Significant changes have taken place in the organisation of the National Health Service in recent years. This volume relates to the situation as it existed in 2005.

ONS performs a statistical analysis on every quarter's notifications. This analysis uses the cumulative sum (CUSUM) technique. This compares the number of notifications in each of the nearly 100 anomalies or groups of anomalies (see **Appendix D**) in each of the areas monitored, with the average number previously reported from that area. If a significant rise is detected in any monitored class or group the relevant health authorities are informed. It must be remembered that an increase in notification may be due to changes in reporting practice rather than due to a true change in prevalence.

From the notification form at **Appendix B**, it can be seen that information is also collected on a number of factors of interest which are not apparently directly relevant to the monitoring, including parents' occupations and mother's age. These factors are used for epidemiological studies.

Although NCAS is primarily for monitoring changes in the frequency of reporting anomalies, it does provide the most extensive data on the prevalence levels available in England and Wales. However the major disadvantage of using the monitoring system to measure prevalence arises from the deficiencies in its coverage. In 1996 the Registrar General's Medical Advisory Committee[1] recommended that '*Where good congenital anomaly registers exist outside OPCS (now ONS) information should be exchanged with these registers*'.

The Welsh Congenital Anomaly Register and Information Service began exchanging data electronically with ONS in 1998[2]. Since then 7 additional local registers have started exchanging data electronically with ONS. The West Midlands Congenital Anomaly Register does not exchange data with ONS.

This annual reference volume includes separate figures for notifications from areas covered by the eight local congenital anomaly registers that exchange data with NCAS (**Tables 1, 8c** and **8d**) and from areas not covered by registers (**Tables 1, 8e** and **8f**).

Table A Local congenital anomaly registers exchanging data electronically with ONS

Year register began exchanging data	Register	Areas included in registers in 2005
1998	Welsh Congenital Anomaly Register and Information Service (CARIS)	Wales
1999	East Midlands and South Yorkshire Congenital Anomaly Register	Derbyshire, Leicestershire, Lincolnshire, Northamptonshire, Nottinghamshire, South Yorkshire, North Lincolnshire Primary Care Trust (PCT), North East Lincolnshire PCT.
2000	North Thames (West) Congenital Malformation Register[2]	Bedfordshire, Hertfordshire, Hillingdon, Barnet, Ealing, Hammersmith and Hounslow, Kensington, Chelsea and Westminster, Brent and Harrow.
2000	Merseyside and Cheshire Congenital Anomaly Survey	Cheshire, Mersey.
2002	Wessex Antenatally Detected Anomalies Register (WANDA)[1]	Hampshire, Isle of Wight, Dorset, South Wiltshire PCT.
2002	Congenital Anomaly Register for Oxfordshire, Berkshire & Buckinghamshire (CAROBB)	Berkshire, Buckinghamshire, Oxfordshire.
2003	Northern Congenital Abnormality Register (NorCas)	Northumberland, Tyne and Wear, County Durham, Tees Valley, Carlisle PCT, Eden Valley PCT, West Cumbria PCT.
2003	South West Congenital Anomaly Register	Avon, Cornwall, Devon, Gloucestershire, Somerset, Wiltshire excluding South Wiltshire PCT.

1 These registers are hospital based. Denominators use area boundaries which are not necessarily exact matches to the areas covered by the registers.

In April 2001, a revised guide for data users and suppliers was distributed.[3] The purpose of this handbook was to provide information about the National System, guidance about reporting anomalies for data suppliers and information about surveillance for health authorities.

Symbols and conventions used

- nil
.. not available
* not available (to protect confidentiality)
In line with the National Statistics Code of Practice and the underpinning Protocol on Data Access and Confidentiality, all statistics in this volume have been disclosure-controlled to protect confidentiality. Thus all subnational numbers smaller than 5 on live and stillborn babies have been suppressed. This disclosure control policy will be revised following the publication of the 'Review of the Dissemination of Health Statistics: Confidentiality Guidance'[4] in October 2006. However, for abortion statistics less than 10 cases have been suppressed (See General notes - abortions, for more details). All rates based on such numbers have also been suppressed. Secondary suppressions have been applied as necessary to avoid the possibility of disclosure through subtraction.

Rates calculated from less than 20 anomalies are distinguished by italic type as a warning to the user that their reliability as a measure may be affected by the small number of events.

References

1. The OPCS Monitoring Scheme for Congenital Malformations. A review of the Registrar General's Medical Advisory Committee. Occasional Paper 43 (1995) HMSO: London.
2. Botting B (2000). The impact of more complete data from Wales on the National Congenital Anomaly System. *Health Statistics Quarterly* **05**, 7-9.
3. Office for National Statistics (2001). *The National Congenital Anomaly System – A guide for data users and suppliers.*
www.statistics.gov.uk/statbase/Product.asp?vlnk=3115
4. Office for National Statistics (2006). *Review of the Dissemination of Health Statistics; Confidentiality Guidance.* http//www.statistics.gov.uk/about/consultations/disclosure.asp

General notes

The statistics in this publication relate to the National Congenital Anomaly System (NCAS) as at 5 September 2006.

Congenital Anomalies

Since 1995 congenital anomaly notifications have been classified to the *International Statistical Classification of Diseases and Related Health Problems* tenth Revision (ICD10). This allowed some conditions which had previously been within a single ICD9 code, to be identified separately, for example *gastroschisis* and *exomphalos* to be shown separately. Details of the ICD10 codes which are included in the major anomaly categories in the tables can be found in **Appendix C**.

Age at death

Stillbirths	late fetal deaths: Until 30 September 1992: after 28 weeks of gestation. From 1 October 1992: after 24 weeks of gestation.
Neonatal deaths	Deaths in the first 4 weeks of life (ie 27 completed days)

Causes of death

Details of causes of death for neonatal deaths and stillbirths in 2005 will be published in Spring 2007 in the ONS publication - Series DH3 Mortality statistics: childhood, infant and perinatal 2005. Figures for 2004 are shown in **Appendix E** for England and Wales - residents only.

It should be noted that revised figures for stillbirths 2004 for England and Wales were published on 30 August 2006. The revision is a consequence of an undercount of stillbirth figures following a failure of some register offices to notify ONS of some stillbirths occurring in their areas.

Abortions

Number of abortions that are shown in **Table 1** have been compiled from notifications of abortions that are completed by the operating practitioners under the 1967 Abortion Act and are sent to the Chief Medical Officers of England and Wales. Section 37 of the Human Fertilisation and Embryology Act 1990 made changes to the Abortion Act 1967. These changes came into effect on 1 April 1991 and principally altered the statutory grounds under which abortions may be performed, and the time limit within which they may be carried out.

A legally induced abortion must be:

a) performed by a registered medical practitioner,
b) performed except in an emergency, in a National Health Service hospital or in a place approved for the purpose of the Act, and
c) certified by two registered medical practitioners as necessary on any of the grounds:

A   the continuance of the pregnancy would involve a risk to the life of the pregnant woman greater than if the pregnancy was terminated;

B   the termination is necessary to prevent grave permanent injury to the health of the pregnant woman;

C   the continuance of the pregnancy would involve risk greater than if the pregnancy were terminated, of injury to the physical or mental health of the pregnant woman;

D   the continuance of the pregnancy would involve risk greater than if the pregnancy were terminated to the physical or mental health of any existing child(ren) of the family of the pregnant woman;

E   there is a substantial risk that if the child were born it would suffer from such physical or mental abnormalities as to be seriously handicapped;

or in an emergency, certified by the operating practitioner as immediately necessary

F   to save the life of the pregnant woman;

or

G   to prevent grave permanent injury to the physical or mental health of the woman.

The abortion notifications reported in this volume are those

The abortion notifications reported in this volume are those carried out under grounds E either alone or in combination with grounds A, B, C or D. The notification form required information about the medical condition found or reported and any diagnosis or suspected condition of the fetus. The medical conditions have been classified to ICD10.

Recommendations from the National Statistics Disclosure Review on abortion statistics

Since April 2002, the Department of Health has been responsible for the processing of the abortions notification forms and information has been made accessible to the Office for National Statistics (ONS) for statistical purposes.

In releasing health statistics, usually with small numbers, there is a risk that it may lead to identifying individuals. To address this, the Department of Health asked the National Statistician to provide guidelines for interpreting the National Statistics Code of Practice and assorted protocols when handling health statistics, in a way that balances data confidentiality risks with the public interest in the use of these figures. In July 2005, ONS published a report on disclosure guidance for abortion statistics. This can be found on the ONS website at:

www.statistics.gov.uk/statbase/Product.asp?vlnk=11988

As recommended by the review, abortion data in **Table 1** and **Appendix E** are suppressed for conditions where there were fewer than 10 cases (ie 0–9 cases).

Area of residence

Tables 5a and **5b** show data by Government Office Region and Strategic Health Authority of residence of mother at the time of the child's birth.

Birthweight

ONS has obtained birthweight for live births since 1975 through the co-operation of district health authorities. Birthweight information given on the birth notification form is transferred from district health authorities to the local registrars of births and deaths who copy it on to the birth registration draft entry forms. These are subsequently forwarded to ONS for statistical processing. A similar system operates for stillbirths, although the initial source of information is the medical certificate which is prepared by the certifying doctor or midwife, and is passed, usually by the parent, to the registrar.

In 2005, 99.8 per cent of live births and 98.4 per cent of stillbirths had a birthweight recorded.

Further information

ONS is happy to provide statistics to outside researchers pursuing related topics subject to the constraints of confidentiality. Particulars relating to individual (anonymous) children are only released with the approval of the data custodian (usually a community paediatrician within the Community Trust), who originally provided the data. Anyone interested in using these data should contact:

Health Analysis Unit
Office for National Statistics
Room 2.164
Government Buildings
Cardiff Road,
Newport,
Gwent
NP10 8XG
Telephone: 01633 813252 or
ncas@ons.gov.uk

Table 1 Summary table showing congenital anomaly statistics from two systems
National Congenital Anomaly System, Abortion Statistics, 2005

England and Wales

Condition	Notifications from areas covered by a local register[3] — Live birth	Notifications from areas covered by a local register[3] — Stillbirth	Notifications from areas not covered by a local register — Live birth	Notifications from areas not covered by a local register — Stillbirth	All areas in England and Wales — Not known[4]	Abortion notifications (under grounds E)[2]
All babies notified	5,173	264	1,419	65	17	1,916
Babies with a mention of:						
Central nervous system anomalies	212	63	70	21	1	456
Anencephalus	7	9	6	3	-	139
All spina bifida	29	5	18	4	-	121
Encephalocele	7	3	3	1	-	24
Congenital hydrocephalus	35	23	18	4	1	44
Eye	74	6	14	3	-	*
Anophthalmia	11	-	4	1	-	*
Cleft lip and palate	374	13	139	2	2	*
Cleft of only lip	86	5	28	-	-	*
Cleft of only palate	151	4	51	-	-	*
Cleft of lip and palate	137	4	60	2	2	*
Other face, ear and neck	109	10	54	3	-	*
Heart and circulatory	1,178	76	132	10	1	111
Respiratory	96	16	13	6	-	19
Alimentary	365	20	60	-	-	*
Tracheo-oesophageal fistula	50	3	3	-	-	*
Oesophageal atresia	12	2	3	-	-	*
Atresia/stenosis large intestine, rectum or anal canal	50	3	12	-	-	*
Genital organs	487	1	135	5	2	*
Hypospadias	383	-	105	-	1	*
Urinary system	684	27	161	6	2	82
Renal agenesis/dygenesis	68	7	19	2	-	25
Epispadias	13	-	2	-	-	*
Musculoskeletal	1,411	85	493	14	6	117
Dislocation of hip	83	-	25	-	-	
Deformities of feet	366	22	170	6	1	*
Polydactyly	239	1	103	-	3	*
Syndactyly	136	4	55	-	-	*
Limb reductions	114	17	41	3	-	11
Diaphragmatic defects	67	11	17	-	-	15
Exomphalos	32	7	11	-	-	13
Gastroschisis	100	2	24	2	-	*
Skin and integument	119	2	71	-	-	*
Chromosomal anomalies	489	68	120	16	4	748
Down syndrome	322	27	97	5	2	429
Endocrine and metabolic disorders	162	4	20	1	-	*
Congenital infections	11	1	-	-	-	*
Other congenital anomalies not elsewhere classified	276	40	102	7	1	60

Sources:
1 National Congenital Anomaly System at 5 September 2006.
2 Department of Health. Abortion Statistics, England and Wales 2005, July 2006.
3 See Introduction for details of areas covered by local congenital anomaly registers.
4 Not known whether live or still birth.

Notes: For more information on stillbirths, neonatal deaths and abortions data: see General notes.

Table 2a 2005 Series MB3 no. 20

Table 2a Live and stillborn babies notified - numbers: sex by condition, 2005

England and Wales

Condition	Total[1]			Live born			Stillborn		
	Total[2]	Male	Female	Total[2]	Male	Female	Total[2]	Male	Female
All babies notified	**6,938**	**4,088**	**2,776**	**6,592**	**3,913**	**2,631**	**329**	**166**	**141**
Babies with mention of:									
Central nervous system anomalies	367	179	179	282	140	141	84	39	38
Anencephalus	25	12	9	13	7	6	12	5	3
All spina bifida	56	26	29	47	23	24	9	3	5
Encephalocele	14	6	8	10	6	4	4	-	4
Congenital hydrocephalus	81	43	36	53	27	26	27	16	10
Eye	97	53	43	88	47	41	9	6	2
Anophthalmia	16	10	6	15	9	6	1	1	-
Cleft lip and palate	530	320	208	513	310	203	15	9	4
Cleft of only lip	119	80	37	114	80	34	5	-	3
Cleft of only palate	206	102	104	202	99	103	4	3	1
Cleft of lip and palate	205	138	67	197	131	66	6	6	-
Other face, ear and neck	176	97	79	163	89	74	13	8	5
Heart and circulatory	1,397	745	643	1,310	694	612	86	50	31
Respiratory	131	69	61	109	60	49	22	9	12
Alimentary	445	278	164	425	269	153	20	9	11
Tracheo-oesophageal fistula	56	34	21	53	34	18	3	-	3
Oesophageal atresia	17	11	6	15	9	6	2	2	-
Atresia/stenosis large intestine, rectum or anal canal	65	41	23	62	39	22	3	2	1
Genital organs	630	555	49	622	553	48	6	1	1
Hypospadias	489	486	1	488	485	1	-	-	-
Urinary system	880	613	257	845	596	243	33	16	14
Renal agenesis/dysgenesis	96	65	28	87	61	24	9	4	4
Epispadias	15	15	-	15	15	-	-	-	-
Musculoskeletal	2,009	1,133	860	1,904	1,076	817	99	53	41
Dislocation of the hip	108	16	92	108	16	92	-	-	-
Deformities of feet	565	324	232	536	306	225	28	17	7
Polydactyly	346	211	134	342	209	132	1	1	-
Syndactyly	195	142	52	191	140	50	4	2	2
Limb reductions	175	100	73	155	91	63	20	9	10
Diaphragmatic defects	95	55	40	84	48	36	11	7	4
Exomphalos	50	32	18	43	28	15	7	4	3
Gastroschisis	128	70	56	124	68	54	4	2	2
Skin and integument	192	92	99	190	91	98	2	1	1
Chromosomal anomalies	697	351	336	609	305	299	84	44	36
Down syndrome	453	249	201	419	227	190	32	21	10
Endocrine and metabolic disorders	187	99	86	182	94	86	5	5	-
Congenital infections	12	5	7	11	5	6	1	-	1
Other congenital anomalies not elsewhere classified	426	223	196	378	202	173	47	20	23
Total live and stillbirths	**649,094**	**332,286**	**316,808**	**645,621**	**330,495**	**315,126**	**3,473**	**1,791**	**1,682**

1 Total includes unknown whether live or stillborn.
2 Includes indeterminate sex and not known/not stated.

Series MB3 no. 20 Table 2b 2005

Table 2b Live and stillborn babies notified - rates per 10,000 live/stillbirths: sex by condition, 2005
England and Wales

Condition	Live born Male	Live born Female	Stillborn Male	Stillborn Female
All babies notified	**118.4**	**83.5**	**926.9**	**838.3**
Babies with mention of:				
Central nervous system anomalies	4.2	4.5	217.8	225.9
Anencephalus	0.2	0.2	27.9	17.8
All spina bifida	0.7	0.8	16.8	29.7
Encephalocele	0.2	0.1	-	23.8
Congenital hydrocephalus	0.8	0.8	89.3	59.5
Eye	1.4	1.3	33.5	11.9
Anophthalmia	0.3	0.2	5.6	-
Cleft lip and palate	9.4	6.4	50.3	23.8
Cleft of only lip	2.4	1.1	-	17.8
Cleft of only palate	3.0	3.3	16.8	5.9
Cleft of lip and palate	4.0	2.1	33.5	-
Other face, ear and neck	2.7	2.3	44.7	29.7
Heart and circulatory	21.0	19.4	279.2	184.3
Respiratory	1.8	1.6	50.3	71.3
Alimentary	8.1	4.9	50.3	65.4
Tracheo-oesophageal fistula	1.0	0.6	-	17.8
Oesophageal atresia	0.3	0.2	11.2	-
Atresia/stenosis large intestine, rectum or anal canal	1.2	0.7	11.2	5.9
Genital organs	16.7	1.5	5.6	5.9
Hypospadias	14.7	0.0	-	-
Urinary system	18.0	7.7	89.3	83.2
Renal agenesis/dysgenesis	1.8	0.8	22.3	23.8
Epispadias	0.5	-	-	-
Musculoskeletal	32.6	25.9	295.9	243.8
Dislocation of the hip	0.5	2.9	-	-
Deformities of feet	9.3	7.1	94.9	41.6
Polydactyly	6.3	4.2	5.6	-
Syndactyly	4.2	1.6	11.2	11.9
Limb reductions	2.8	2.0	50.3	59.5
Diaphragmatic defects	1.5	1.1	39.1	23.8
Exomphalos	0.8	0.5	22.3	17.8
Gastroschisis	2.1	1.7	11.2	11.9
Skin and integument	2.8	3.1	5.6	5.9
Chromosomal anomalies	9.2	9.5	245.7	214.0
Down syndrome	6.9	6.0	117.3	59.5
Endocrine and metabolic disorders	2.8	2.7	27.9	-
Congenital infections	0.2	0.2	-	5.9
Other congenital anomalies not elsewhere classified	6.1	5.5	111.7	136.7

Table 3 2005 Series MB3 no.20

Table 3   All babies notified - numbers: England and Wales
          number of reported anomalies, 2005

All babies notified	6,938
1 anomaly	5,485
2 anomalies	936
3 anomalies	283
4 anomalies	128
5 anomalies	51
6 anomalies	31
7 anomalies	11
8 or more anomalies	13

Series MB3 no.20 Tables 4a and 4b 2005

Table 4a Live and stillborn babies notified - numbers: multiplicity by condition, 2005 — England and Wales

Condition	Total[1] Total[2]	Singleton	Multiple	Live born Total[2]	Singleton	Multiple	Stillborn Total[2]	Singleton	Multiple
All babies notified	**6,938**	6,347	259	6,592	6,042	223	329	291	36
Babies with mention of:									
Central nervous system anomalies	367	335	29	282	263	16	84	71	13
Anencephalus	25	17	8	13	10	3	12	7	5
All spina bifida	56	54	2	47	46	1	9	8	1
Eye	97	87	3	88	79	2	9	8	1
Cleft lip and palate	530	509	14	513	493	13	15	14	1
Other face, ear and neck	176	162	3	163	152	1	13	10	2
Heart and circulatory	1,397	1,281	71	1,310	1,206	60	86	74	11
Respiratory	131	118	3	109	96	3	22	22	-
Alimentary	445	386	23	425	368	21	20	18	2
Genital organs	630	544	30	622	537	30	6	6	-
Urinary system	880	786	28	845	755	27	33	31	1
Musculoskeletal	2,009	1,860	63	1,904	1,761	57	99	93	6
Skin and integument	192	180	7	190	178	7	2	2	-
Chromosomal anomalies	697	657	25	609	580	14	84	73	11
Down syndrome	453	425	17	419	397	11	32	26	6
Endocrine and metabolic disorders	187	176	9	182	172	8	5	4	1
Congenital infections	12	12	-	11	11	-	1	1	-
Other congenital anomalies not elsewhere classified	426	400	17	378	359	10	47	40	7
Total live and stillbirths	**649,094**	629,883	19,211	645,621	626,668	18,953	3,473	3,215	258

1 Total includes unknown whether live or stillborn.
2 Includes not known/not stated.

Table 4b Live and stillborn babies notified - rates per 10,000 live/stillbirths: multiplicity by condition, 2005 — England and Wales

Condition	Total[1] Total[2]	Singleton	Multiple	Live born Total[2]	Singleton	Multiple	Stillborn Total[2]	Singleton	Multiple
All babies notified	**106.9**	100.8	134.8	102.1	96.4	117.7	947.3	905.1	1395.3
Babies with mention of:									
Central nervous system anomalies	5.7	5.3	15.1	4.4	4.2	8.4	241.9	220.8	503.9
Anencephalus	0.4	0.3	4.2	0.2	0.2	1.6	34.6	21.8	193.8
All spina bifida	0.9	0.9	1.0	0.7	0.7	0.5	25.9	24.9	38.8
Eye	1.5	1.4	1.6	1.4	1.3	1.1	25.9	24.9	38.8
Cleft lip and palate	8.2	8.1	7.3	7.9	7.9	6.9	43.2	43.5	38.8
Other face, ear and neck	2.7	2.6	1.6	2.5	2.4	0.5	37.4	31.1	77.5
Heart and circulatory	21.5	20.3	37.0	20.3	19.2	31.7	247.6	230.2	426.4
Respiratory	2.0	1.9	1.6	1.7	1.5	1.6	63.3	68.4	-
Alimentary	6.9	6.1	12.0	6.6	5.9	11.1	57.6	56.0	77.5
Genital organs	9.7	8.6	15.6	9.6	8.6	15.8	17.3	18.7	-
Urinary system	13.6	12.5	14.6	13.1	12.0	14.2	95.0	96.4	38.8
Musculoskeletal	31.0	29.5	32.8	29.5	28.1	30.1	285.1	289.3	232.6
Skin and integument	3.0	2.9	3.6	2.9	2.8	3.7	5.8	6.2	-
Chromosomal anomalies	10.7	10.4	13.0	9.4	9.3	7.4	241.9	227.1	426.4
Down syndrome	7.0	6.7	8.8	6.5	6.3	5.8	92.1	80.9	232.6
Endocrine and metabolic disorders	2.9	2.8	4.7	2.8	2.7	4.2	14.4	12.4	38.8
Congenital infections	0.2	0.2	-	0.2	0.2	-	2.9	3.1	-
Other congenital anomalies not elsewhere classified	6.6	6.4	8.8	5.9	5.7	5.3	135.3	124.4	271.3

1 Total includes unknown whether live or stillborn.
2 Includes not known/not stated.

Table 5a 2005 Series MB3 no.20

Table 5a Total (live and still) births, all babies notified - numbers:
condition by area of usual residence of mother, 2005

Area of usual residence	Total (live and still) births	Central nervous system anomalies	Cleft lip and palate	Other face, ear and neck	Heart and circulatory	Alimentary	Genital organs
ENGLAND AND WALES	**649,094**	**367**	**530**	**176**	**1,397**	**445**	**630**
England	**616,326**	**339**	**477**	**160**	**1,085**	**398**	**594**
Wales[1]	**32,768**	**28**	**53**	**16**	**312**	**47**	**36**
Government Office Regions							
North East[1]	28,411	28	49	*	231	32	20
North West	82,175	59	81	19	111	32	83
Yorkshire and The Humber	61,044	28	48	15	91	24	66
East Midlands[1]	49,325	38	61	20	96	56	91
West Midlands	66,350	18	21	*	28	9	20
East	64,969	30	52	20	59	21	47
London	116,721	45	40	18	106	32	79
South East	94,375	41	73	15	116	72	52
South West[1]	52,956	52	52	42	247	120	136
Strategic Health Authorities/ Government Regions							
North East							
County Durham and Tees Valley[1]	13,335	15	28	*	86	10	*
Northumberland, Tyne and Wear[1]	15,076	13	21	*	145	22	*
North West							
Cheshire and Merseyside[1]	26,500	30	28	*	38	18	39
Cumbria and Lancashire	21,922	11	25	*	34	9	21
Greater Manchester	33,753	18	28	10	39	5	23
Yorkshire and The Humber							
North and East Yorkshire and Northern Lincolnshire	17,528	*	17	*	*	*	12
South Yorkshire[1]	15,169	13	21	7	65	15	44
West Yorkshire	28,347	*	10	*	*	*	10
East Midlands							
Leicestershire, Northamptonshire and Rutland[1]	19,985	15	26	8	42	23	32
Trent[1]	29,340	23	35	12	54	33	59
West Midlands							
Birmingham and the Black Country	32,374	*	*	*	8	5	9
Shropshire and Staffordshire	16,736	7	10	*	12	*	*
West Midlands South	17,240	*	*	*	8	*	*
East							
Bedfordshire and Hertfordshire[1]	21,153	*	22	*	41	12	22
Essex	19,157	*	10	*	*	*	11
Norfolk, Suffolk and Cambridgeshire	24,659	17	20	11	*	*	14
London							
North Central London	19,032	6	6	*	10	9	11
North East London	26,981	*	*	*	*	*	*
North West London[1]	27,321	35	30	10	87	19	50
South East London	24,197	*	*	*	*	*	8
South West London	19,190	*	*	*	9	*	*
South East							
Hampshire and Isle of Wight[1]	19,948	*	17	*	52	24	13
Kent and Medway	18,833	*	6	*	*	5	6
Surrey and Sussex	28,296	8	16	7	*	16	12
Thames Valley[1]	27,298	27	34	5	46	27	21
South West							
Avon, Gloucestershire and Wiltshire[1]	25,508	24	23	20	98	58	77
Dorset and Somerset[1]	11,761	14	10	7	29	12	15
South West Peninsula[1]	15,687	14	19	15	120	50	44

1 Area wholly covered by a local congenital anomaly register that exchanges data with ONS - see Introduction table A

Series MB3 no.20 Table 5a 2005

England and Wales

Urinary system	Musculoskeletal	Skin and integument	Chromosomal anomalies	Down syndrome	Endocrine and metabolic disorders	Other congenital anomalies not elsewhere classified	Area of usual residence
880	2,009	192	697	453	187	426	**ENGLAND AND WALES**
800	1,845	173	601	410	158	373	England
80	164	19	96	43	29	53	Wales[1]
							Government Office Regions
46	61	*	50	34	9	14	North East[1]
155	246	24	79	55	12	54	North West
37	141	15	33	26	26	23	Yorkshire and The Humber
126	264	30	80	47	55	38	East Midlands[1]
37	84	*	23	15	8	16	West Midlands
56	151	20	58	39	*	33	East
69	267	34	63	47	*	48	London
101	237	22	128	92	13	76	South East
173	394	22	87	55	28	71	South West[1]
							Strategic Health Authorities/ Government Regions
							North East
25	29	*	22	16	*	7	County Durham and Tees Valley[1]
21	32	*	28	18	*	7	Northumberland, Tyne and Wear[1]
							North West
103	84	6	27	16	*	23	Cheshire and Merseyside[1]
11	49	11	29	20	*	11	Cumbria and Lancashire
41	113	7	23	19	5	20	Greater Manchester
							Yorkshire and The Humber
*	51	8	*	*	*	11	North and East Yorkshire and Northern Lincolnshire
20	69	*	20	16	21	*	South Yorkshire[1]
*	21	*	*	*	*	*	West Yorkshire
							East Midlands
78	107	11	28	16	17	15	Leicestershire, Northamptonshire and Rutland[1]
48	157	19	52	31	38	23	Trent[1]
							West Midlands
18	38	*	5	*	*	10	Birmingham and the Black Country
14	23	*	12	6	*	*	Shropshire and Staffordshire
5	23	*	6	*	*	*	West Midlands South
							East
27	62	*	36	23	*	11	Bedfordshire and Hertfordshire[1]
9	34	*	9	8	*	13	Essex
20	55	9	13	8	*	9	Norfolk, Suffolk and Cambridgeshire
							London
7	38	*	13	11	*	*	North Central London
*	19	*	*	*	*	*	North East London
54	170	*	44	31	*	28	North West London[1]
*	20	24	*	*	*	7	South East London
6	20	*	6	5	*	6	South West London
							South East
*	63	*	43	29	9	21	Hampshire and Isle of Wight[1]
*	21	*	*	*	*	*	Kent and Medway
32	61	6	*	*	*	*	Surrey and Sussex
47	92	8	60	45	*	34	Thames Valley[1]
							South West
109	164	*	43	27	*	33	Avon, Gloucestershire and Wiltshire[1]
22	61	*	13	6	*	11	Dorset and Somerset[1]
42	169	11	31	22	14	27	South West Peninsula[1]

Table 5b 2005 Series MB3 no.20

Table 5b All babies notified - rates per 10,000 total births:
condition by area of usual residence of mother, 2005

Area of usual residence

	Central nervous system anomalies	Cleft lip and palate	Other face, ear and neck	Heart and circulatory	Alimentary	Genital organs
ENGLAND AND WALES	5.7	8.2	2.7	21.5	6.9	9.7
England	5.5	7.7	2.6	17.6	6.5	9.6
Wales[1]	8.5	16.2	4.9	95.2	14.3	11.0
Government Office Regions						
North East[1]	9.9	17.2	*	81.3	11.3	7.0
North West	7.2	9.9	2.3	13.5	3.9	10.1
Yorkshire and The Humber	4.6	7.9	2.5	14.9	3.9	10.8
East Midlands[1]	7.7	12.4	4.1	19.5	11.4	18.4
West Midlands	2.7	3.2	*	4.2	1.4	3.0
East	4.6	8.0	3.1	9.1	3.2	7.2
London	3.9	3.4	1.5	9.1	2.7	6.8
South East	4.3	7.7	1.6	12.3	7.6	5.5
South West[1]	9.8	9.8	7.9	46.6	22.7	25.7

1 Area wholly covered by a local congenital anomaly register that exchanges data with ONS - see Introduction table A

England and Wales

Area of usual residence

Urinary system	Musculoskeletal	Skin and integument	Chromosomal anomalies	Down syndrome	Congenital metabolic disorders	Other congenital anomalies not elsewhere classified	
13.6	**31.0**	**3.0**	**10.7**	**7.0**	**2.9**	**6.6**	**ENGLAND AND WALES**
13.0	**29.9**	**2.8**	**9.8**	**6.7**	**2.6**	**6.1**	**England**
24.4	**50.0**	*5.8*	**29.3**	**13.1**	**8.9**	**16.2**	**Wales**
							Government Office Regions
16.2	21.5	*	17.6	12.0	*3.2*	*4.9*	North East[1]
18.9	29.9	2.9	9.6	6.7	*1.5*	6.6	North West
6.1	23.1	*2.5*	5.4	4.3	4.3	3.8	Yorkshire and The Humber
25.5	53.5	6.1	16.2	9.5	11.2	7.7	East Midlands[1]
5.6	12.7	*	3.5	2.3	*1.2*	*2.4*	West Midlands
8.6	23.2	3.1	8.9	6.0	*	5.1	East
5.9	22.9	2.9	5.4	4.0	*	4.1	London
10.7	25.1	2.3	13.6	9.7	*1.4*	8.1	South East
32.7	74.4	4.2	16.4	10.4	5.3	13.4	South West[1]

Tables 6a and 6b 2005 Series MB3 no.20

Table 6a   All babies notified - numbers:
              month of birth by condition, 2005

Condition	Total	January	February	March	April	May	June
All babies notified	**6,938**	**635**	**547**	**645**	**630**	**572**	**560**
Babies with mention of:							
Central nervous system anomalies	367	28	31	26	29	47	34
Anencephalus	25	4	-	3	2	3	2
All spina bifida	56	2	7	7	4	7	5
Eye	97	9	9	11	7	8	11
Cleft lip and palate	530	56	36	47	36	42	47
Other face, ear and neck	176	19	18	14	16	15	13
Heart and circulatory	1,397	150	111	132	128	122	105
Respiratory	131	12	11	17	8	12	10
Alimentary	445	35	29	44	31	53	32
Genital organs	630	52	55	47	62	45	49
Urinary system	880	76	65	82	85	66	83
Musculoskeletal	2,009	171	163	186	198	158	153
Skin and integument	192	11	12	19	7	13	16
Chromosomal anomalies	697	67	52	62	62	53	53
Down syndrome	453	45	36	44	39	31	37
Endocrine and metabolic disorders	187	23	12	16	20	12	17
Congenital infections	12	1	-	2	3	1	1
Other congenital anomalies not elsewhere classified	426	47	35	43	36	40	43
Total live and stillbirths	**649,094**	**52,784**	**48,350**	**53,894**	**52,332**	**53,922**	**54,376**

Table 6b   All babies notified - rates per 10,000 total births:
              month of birth by condition, 2005

Condition	Total	January	February	March	April	May	June
All babies notified	**106.9**	120.3	113.1	119.7	120.4	106.1	103.0
Babies with mention of:							
Central nervous system anomalies	5.7	5.3	6.4	4.8	5.5	8.7	6.3
Anencephalus	0.4	0.8	-	0.6	0.4	0.6	0.4
All spina bifida	0.9	0.4	1.4	1.3	0.8	1.3	0.9
Eye	1.5	1.7	1.9	2.0	1.3	1.5	2.0
Cleft lip and palate	8.2	10.6	7.4	8.7	6.9	7.8	8.6
Other face, ear and neck	2.7	3.6	3.7	2.6	3.1	2.8	2.4
Heart and circulatory	21.5	28.4	23.0	24.5	24.5	22.6	19.3
Respiratory	2.0	2.3	2.3	3.2	1.5	2.2	1.8
Alimentary	6.9	6.6	6.0	8.2	5.9	9.8	5.9
Genital organs	9.7	9.9	11.4	8.7	11.8	8.3	9.0
Urinary system	13.6	14.4	13.4	15.2	16.2	12.2	15.3
Musculoskeletal	31.0	32.4	33.7	34.5	37.8	29.3	28.1
Skin and integument	3.0	2.1	2.5	3.5	1.3	2.4	2.9
Chromosomal anomalies	10.7	12.7	10.8	11.5	11.8	9.8	9.7
Down syndrome	7.0	8.5	7.4	8.2	7.5	5.7	6.8
Endocrine and metabolic disorders	2.9	4.4	2.5	3.0	3.8	2.2	3.1
Congenital infections	0.2	0.2	-	0.4	0.6	0.2	0.2
Other congenital anomalies not elsewhere classified	6.6	8.9	7.2	8.0	6.9	7.4	7.9

Series MB3 no.20 Tables 6a and 6b 2005

England and Wales

Month of birth						Condition
July	August	September	October	November	December	
608	**601**	**574**	**584**	**510**	**472**	**All babies notified**
						Babies with mention of:
38	34	30	29	18	23	**Central nervous system anomalies**
2	3	2	3	-	1	Anencephalus
4	5	6	3	2	4	All spina bifida
8	9	7	8	6	4	**Eye**
37	67	53	39	32	38	**Cleft lip and palate**
5	20	18	8	14	16	**Other face, ear and neck**
121	117	102	124	95	90	**Heart and circulatory**
8	10	13	10	9	11	**Respiratory**
34	39	40	42	32	34	**Alimentary**
57	64	54	66	42	37	**Genital organs**
83	64	77	71	69	59	**Urinary system**
168	193	161	166	150	142	**Musculoskeletal**
13	11	22	29	21	18	**Skin and integument**
76	62	50	49	59	52	**Chromosomal anomalies**
49	43	22	33	38	36	Down syndrome
17	13	20	9	13	15	**Endocrine and metabolic disorders**
2	-	-	-	2	-	**Congenital infections**
40	31	28	39	19	25	**Other congenital anomalies not elsewhere classified**
56,802	**57,527**	**56,660**	**55,903**	**52,513**	**54,031**	**Total live and stillbirths**

England and Wales

Month of birth						Condition
July	August	September	October	November	December	
107.0	104.5	101.3	104.5	97.1	87.4	**All babies notified**
						Babies with mention of:
6.7	5.9	5.3	5.2	3.4	4.3	**Central nervous system anomalies**
0.4	0.5	0.4	0.5	-	0.2	Anencephalus
0.7	0.9	1.1	0.5	0.4	0.7	All spina bifida
1.4	1.6	1.2	1.4	1.1	0.7	**Eye**
6.5	11.6	9.4	7.0	6.1	7.0	**Cleft lip and palate**
0.9	3.5	3.2	1.4	2.7	3.0	**Other face, ear and neck**
21.3	20.3	18.0	22.2	18.1	16.7	**Heart and circulatory**
1.4	1.7	2.3	1.8	1.7	2.0	**Respiratory**
6.0	6.8	7.1	7.5	6.1	6.3	**Alimentary**
10.0	11.1	9.5	11.8	8.0	6.8	**Genital organs**
14.6	11.1	13.6	12.7	13.1	10.9	**Urinary system**
29.6	33.5	28.4	29.7	28.6	26.3	**Musculoskeletal**
2.3	1.9	3.9	5.2	4.0	3.3	**Skin and integument**
13.4	10.8	8.8	8.8	11.2	9.6	**Chromosomal anomalies**
8.6	7.5	3.9	5.9	7.2	6.7	Down syndrome
3.0	2.3	3.5	1.6	2.5	2.8	**Endocrine and metabolic disorders**
0.4	-	-	-	0.4	-	**Congenital infections**
7.0	5.4	4.9	7.0	3.6	4.6	**Other congenital anomalies not elsewhere classified**

Table 7a 2005 Series MB3 no.20

Table 7a Live and stillborn babies notified - numbers: birthweight by condition, 2005

England and Wales

Condition			Total[1]	500-999	1,000-1,499	1,500-1,999	2,000-2,499	2,500-2,999	3,000-3,499	3,500 and over	Not stated
All babies notified	Total[2]	a	6,938	149	182	294	521	1,189	1,793	1,738	1,030
	Live born	b	6,592	78	129	249	494	1,166	1,776	1,728	958
	Stillborn	c	329	71	53	44	27	20	14	7	66
Babies with mention of:											
Central nervous system anomalies		a	367	29	28	36	30	66	57	61	51
		b	282	4	11	26	25	63	55	60	34
		c	84	25	17	10	5	3	2	1	16
Anencephalus		a	25	4	4	2	4	4	1	1	3
		b	13	-	2	1	3	4	1	1	-
		c	12	4	2	1	1	-	-	-	3
All spina bifida		a	56	-	2	5	3	14	13	9	9
		b	47	-	-	2	3	14	13	9	5
		c	9	-	2	3	-	-	-	-	4
Eye		a	97	1	4	5	12	19	23	20	12
		b	88	-	1	5	11	18	21	20	12
		c	9	1	3	-	1	1	2	-	-
Cleft lip and palate		a	530	8	13	19	33	95	147	152	62
		b	513	6	9	18	32	94	145	152	57
		c	15	2	4	1	1	-	1	-	5
Other face, ear and neck		a	176	8	5	6	15	31	53	40	15
		b	163	5	2	6	14	31	52	40	13
		c	13	3	3	-	1	-	1	-	2
Heart and circulatory		a	1,397	50	59	81	122	228	283	242	317
		b	1,310	31	47	68	115	223	280	240	301
		c	86	19	12	13	7	5	3	2	15
Respiratory		a	131	7	7	7	15	23	20	26	23
		b	109	5	4	3	11	19	18	26	23
		c	22	2	3	4	4	4	2	-	-
Alimentary		a	445	12	16	30	55	78	98	82	73
		b	425	5	14	28	54	75	97	82	70
		c	20	7	2	2	1	3	1	-	3
Genital organs		a	630	7	15	30	53	104	163	209	48
		b	622	5	15	28	53	102	163	209	47
		c	6	2	-	1	-	2	-	-	-
Urinary system		a	880	14	4	33	45	131	252	269	128
		b	845	7	3	26	41	127	250	268	122
		c	33	7	1	7	4	3	2	-	6
Musculoskeletal		a	2,009	46	47	76	162	379	557	538	189
		b	1,904	25	32	68	154	373	550	535	166
		c	99	21	15	8	8	6	5	3	20
Skin and integument		a	192	2	1	6	9	37	81	50	6
		b	190	1	1	6	9	37	80	50	6
		c	2	1	-	-	-	-	1	-	-
Chromosomal anomalies		a	697	29	25	47	78	132	129	80	169
		b	609	13	10	34	73	128	127	77	145
		c	84	16	15	13	5	3	2	2	22
Down syndrome		a	453	12	8	23	54	107	104	59	85
		b	419	6	5	15	52	104	103	58	76
		c	32	6	3	8	2	2	1	1	8
Endocrine and metabolic disorders		a	187	6	9	7	16	31	49	46	22
		b	182	5	8	6	16	31	49	46	21
		c	5	1	1	1	-	-	-	-	1
Congenital infections		a	12	-	-	1	4	2	1	3	1
		b	11	-	-	-	4	2	1	3	1
		c	1	-	-	1	-	-	-	-	-
Other congenital anomalies not elsewhere classified		a	426	14	16	32	40	64	93	100	62
		b	378	4	9	23	38	60	90	99	54
		c	47	10	7	9	2	4	3	-	8
Total live and stillbirths		a	649,094	4,324	5,251	10,314	31,157	109,841	230,326	255,587	2,294
Live born		b	645,621	3,203	4,816	9,941	30,774	109,423	229,936	255,290	2,238
Stillborn		c	3,473	1,121	435	373	383	418	390	297	56

1 Total includes under 500 grammes.
2 Total includes unknown whether live or stillborn.

Table 7b Live and stillborn babies notified - rates per 10,000 live/stillbirths: birthweight by condition, 2005

England and Wales

Condition			Birthweight (grammes)							
			Total[1]	500-999	1,000-1,499	1,500-1,999	2,000-2,499	2,500-2,999	3,000-3,499	3,500 and over
All babies notified	Live born	a	102.1	243.5	267.9	250.5	160.5	106.6	77.2	67.7
	Stillborn	b	947.3	633.4	1218.4	1179.6	705.0	478.5	359.0	235.7
Babies with mention of:										
Central nervous system anomalies		a	4.4	12.5	22.8	26.2	8.1	5.8	2.4	2.4
		b	241.9	223.0	390.8	268.1	130.5	71.8	51.3	33.7
Anencephalus		a	0.2	-	4.2	1.0	1.0	0.4	0.0	0.0
		b	34.6	35.7	46.0	26.8	26.1	-	-	-
All spina bifida		a	0.7	-	-	2.0	1.0	1.3	0.6	0.4
		b	25.9	-	46.0	80.4	-	-	-	-
Eye		a	1.4	-	2.1	5.0	3.6	1.6	0.9	0.8
		b	25.9	8.9	69.0	-	26.1	23.9	51.3	-
Cleft lip and palate		a	7.9	18.7	18.7	18.1	10.4	8.6	6.3	6.0
		b	43.2	17.8	92.0	26.8	26.1	-	25.6	-
Other face, ear and neck		a	2.5	15.6	4.2	6.0	4.5	2.8	2.3	1.6
		b	37.4	26.8	69.0	-	26.1	-	25.6	-
Heart and circulatory		a	20.3	96.8	97.6	68.4	37.4	20.4	12.2	9.4
		b	247.6	169.5	275.9	348.5	182.8	119.6	76.9	67.3
Respiratory		a	1.7	15.6	8.3	3.0	3.6	1.7	0.8	1.0
		b	63.3	17.8	69.0	107.2	104.4	95.7	51.3	-
Alimentary		a	6.6	15.6	29.1	28.2	17.5	6.9	4.2	3.2
		b	57.6	62.4	46.0	53.6	26.1	71.8	25.6	-
Genital organs		a	9.6	15.6	31.1	28.2	17.2	9.3	7.1	8.2
		b	17.3	17.8	-	26.8	-	47.8	-	-
Urinary system		a	13.1	21.9	6.2	26.2	13.3	11.6	10.9	10.5
		b	95.0	62.4	23.0	187.7	104.4	71.8	51.3	-
Musculoskeletal		a	29.5	78.1	66.4	68.4	50.0	34.1	23.9	21.0
		b	285.1	187.3	344.8	214.5	208.9	143.5	128.2	101.0
Skin and integument		a	2.9	3.1	2.1	6.0	2.9	3.4	3.5	2.0
		b	5.8	8.9	-	-	-	-	25.6	-
Chromosomal anomalies		a	9.4	40.6	20.8	34.2	23.7	11.7	5.5	3.0
		b	241.9	142.7	344.8	348.5	130.5	71.8	51.3	67.3
Down syndrome		a	6.5	18.7	10.4	15.1	16.9	9.5	4.5	2.3
		b	92.1	53.5	69.0	214.5	52.2	47.8	25.6	33.7
Endocrine and metabolic disorders		a	2.8	15.6	16.6	6.0	5.2	2.8	2.1	1.8
		b	14.4	8.9	23.0	26.8	-	-	-	-
Congenital infections		a	0.2	-	-	-	1.3	0.2	0.0	0.1
		b	2.9	-	-	26.8	-	-	-	-
Other congenital anomalies not elsewhere classified		a	5.9	12.5	18.7	23.1	12.3	5.5	3.9	3.9
		b	135.3	89.2	160.9	241.3	52.2	95.7	76.9	-

1 Total includes under 500 grammes.

Tables 8a and 8b 2005 Series MB3 no.20

Table 8a All babies notified - numbers: age of mother by condition, 2005

England and Wales

Condition	Total[1]	Under 20	20-24	25-29	30-34	35-39	40-44	45 and over
All babies notified	6,938	506	1,276	1,670	1,824	1,178	302	27
Babies with mention of:								
Central nervous system anomalies	367	27	99	82	88	60	10	-
Anencephalus	25	1	7	5	8	3	1	-
All spina bifida	56	4	17	12	14	8	1	-
Eye	97	3	17	23	33	19	-	1
Cleft lip and palate	530	32	108	123	143	82	18	4
Other face, ear and neck	176	10	36	36	47	35	10	-
Heart and circulatory	1,397	116	240	339	348	243	67	9
Respiratory	131	5	30	26	37	27	4	-
Alimentary	445	36	77	98	131	79	12	3
Genital organs	630	29	127	162	163	116	23	-
Urinary system	880	58	155	226	253	136	39	1
Musculoskeletal	2,009	180	392	493	521	330	66	7
Skin and integument	192	12	26	58	62	30	2	-
Chromosomal anomalies	697	32	69	97	155	202	90	15
Down syndrome	453	15	42	52	97	147	68	10
Endocrine and metabolic disorders	187	13	40	50	35	31	7	1
Congenital infections	12	2	2	3	2	3	-	-
Other congenital anomalies not elsewhere classified	426	27	86	100	116	70	17	3
Total live and stillbirths	649,094	45,107	122,748	165,160	188,999	104,688	21,288	1,104

1 Totals include age not stated

Table 8b All babies notified - rates per 10,000 total births: age of mother by condition, 2005

England and Wales

Condition	Total[1]	Under 20	20-24	25-29	30-34	35-39	40-44	45 and over
All babies notified	106.9	112.2	104.0	101.1	96.5	112.5	141.9	244.6
Babies with metnion of:								
Central nervous system anomalies	5.7	6.0	8.1	5.0	4.7	5.7	4.7	-
Anencephalus	0.4	0.2	0.6	0.3	0.4	0.3	0.5	-
All spina bifida	0.9	0.9	1.4	0.7	0.7	0.8	0.5	-
Eye	1.5	0.7	1.4	1.4	1.7	1.8	-	9.1
Cleft lip and palate	8.2	7.1	8.8	7.4	7.6	7.8	8.5	36.2
Other face, ear and neck	2.7	2.2	2.9	2.2	2.5	3.3	4.7	-
Heart and circulatory	21.5	25.7	19.6	20.5	18.4	23.2	31.5	81.5
Respiratory	2.0	1.1	2.4	1.6	2.0	2.6	1.9	-
Alimentary	6.9	8.0	6.3	5.9	6.9	7.5	5.6	27.2
Genital organs	9.7	6.4	10.3	9.8	8.6	11.1	10.8	-
Urinary system	13.6	12.9	12.6	13.7	13.4	13.0	18.3	9.1
Musculoskeletal	31.0	39.9	31.9	29.8	27.6	31.5	31.0	63.4
Skin and integument	3.0	2.7	2.1	3.5	3.3	2.9	0.9	-
Chromosomal anomalies	10.7	7.1	5.6	5.9	8.2	19.3	42.3	135.9
Down syndrome	7.0	3.3	3.4	3.1	5.1	14.0	31.9	90.6
Endocrine and metabolic disorders	2.9	2.9	3.3	3.0	1.9	3.0	3.3	9.1
Congenital infections	0.2	0.4	0.2	0.2	0.1	0.3	-	-
Other congenital anomalies not elsewhere classified	6.6	6.0	7.0	6.1	6.1	6.7	8.0	27.2

1 Totals include age not stated.

Tables 8c and 8d 2005 Series MB3 no.20

Table 8c All babies notified - numbers: age of mother by condition, 2005

Areas covered by a local register in England and Wales[1]

Condition	Total[2]	Under 20	20-24	25-29	30-34	35-39	40 and over
All babies notified	**5,444**	**395**	**1,005**	**1,286**	**1,455**	**931**	**255**
Babies with a mention of:							
Central nervous system anomalies	**276**	**17**	**75**	**62**	**69**	**45**	**7**
Anencephalus	16	1	5	5	4	1	0
All spina bifida	34	2	11	7	8	6	0
Eye	**80**	**2**	**15**	**20**	**25**	**17**	**1**
Cleft lip and palate	**387**	**21**	**85**	**87**	**100**	**63**	**16**
Other face, ear and neck	**119**	**6**	**23**	**23**	**33**	**25**	**7**
Heart and circulatory	**1,255**	**101**	**225**	**305**	**310**	**218**	**65**
Respiratory	**112**	**4**	**27**	**24**	**31**	**21**	**3**
Alimentary	**385**	**34**	**67**	**84**	**109**	**70**	**12**
Genital organs	**488**	**24**	**96**	**124**	**133**	**88**	**17**
Urinary system	**711**	**46**	**124**	**180**	**208**	**116**	**31**
Musculoskeletal	**1,501**	**138**	**294**	**352**	**407**	**243**	**58**
Skin and integument	**121**	**10**	**15**	**33**	**39**	**21**	**1**
Chromosomal anomalies	**559**	**25**	**53**	**80**	**132**	**157**	**80**
Down syndrome	350	11	31	43	79	109	58
Endocrine and metabolic disorders	**166**	**10**	**37**	**46**	**29**	**27**	**7**
Congenital infections	**12**	**2**	**2**	**3**	**2**	**3**	**0**
Other congenital anomalies not elsewhere classified	316	19	62	69	89	56	17
Total live and stillbirths	**312,110**	**22,166**	**58,406**	**78,768**	**91,403**	**50,630**	**10,737**

1 See Introduction for details of areas covered by a local register.
2 Totals include age not stated.

Table 8d All babies notified - rates per 10,000 total births: age of mother by condition, 2005

Areas covered by a local register in England and Wales[1]

Condition	Total[2]	Under 20	20-24	25-29	30-34	35-39	40 and over
All babies notified	**174.4**	**178.2**	**172.1**	**163.3**	**159.2**	**183.9**	**237.5**
Babies with a mention of:							
Central nervous system anomalies	**8.8**	*7.7*	*12.8*	*7.9*	*7.5*	*8.9*	*6.5*
Anencephalus	*0.5*	*0.5*	*0.9*	*0.6*	*0.4*	*0.2*	*0.0*
All spina bifida	*1.1*	*0.9*	*1.9*	*0.9*	*0.9*	*1.2*	*0.0*
Eye	**2.6**	*0.9*	*2.6*	*2.5*	*2.7*	*3.4*	*0.9*
Cleft lip and palate	**12.4**	*9.5*	*14.6*	*11.0*	*10.9*	*12.4*	*14.9*
Other face, ear and neck	**3.8**	*2.7*	*3.9*	*2.9*	*3.6*	*4.9*	*6.5*
Heart and circulatory	**40.2**	*45.6*	*38.5*	*38.7*	*33.9*	*43.1*	*60.5*
Respiratory	**3.6**	*1.8*	*4.6*	*3.0*	*3.4*	*4.1*	*2.8*
Alimentary	**12.3**	*15.3*	*11.5*	*10.7*	*11.9*	*13.8*	*11.2*
Genital organs	**15.6**	*10.8*	*16.4*	*15.7*	*14.6*	*17.4*	*15.8*
Urinary system	**22.8**	*20.8*	*21.2*	*22.9*	*22.8*	*22.9*	*28.9*
Musculoskeletal	**48.1**	*62.3*	*50.3*	*44.7*	*44.5*	*48.0*	*54.0*
Skin and integument	**3.9**	*4.5*	*2.6*	*4.2*	*4.3*	*4.1*	*0.9*
Chromosomal anomalies	**17.9**	*11.3*	*9.1*	*10.2*	*14.4*	*31.0*	*74.5*
Down syndrome	**11.2**	*5.0*	*5.3*	*5.5*	*8.6*	*21.5*	*54.0*
Endocrine and metabolic disorders	**5.3**	*4.5*	*6.3*	*5.8*	*3.2*	*5.3*	*6.5*
Congenital infections	*0.4*	*0.9*	*0.3*	*0.4*	*0.2*	*0.6*	*0.0*
Other congenital anomalies not elsewhere classified	**10.1**	*8.6*	*10.6*	*8.8*	*9.7*	*11.1*	*15.8*

1 See Introduction for details of areas covered by a local register.
2 Totals include age not stated.

Tables 8e and 8f 2005 Series MB3 no.20

Table 8e   All babies notified - numbers: age of mother by condition, 2005

Areas not covered by a register in England and Wales[1]

Condition	Age of mother						
	Total[2]	Under 20	20-24	25-29	30-34	35-39	40 and over
All babies notified	**1,494**	**111**	**271**	**384**	**369**	**247**	**74**
Babies with a mention of:							
Central nervous system anomalies	91	10	24	20	19	15	3
Anencephalus	9	0	2	0	4	2	1
All spina bifida	22	2	6	5	6	2	1
Eye	17	1	2	3	8	2	0
Cleft lip and palate	143	11	23	36	43	19	6
Other face, ear and neck	57	4	13	13	14	10	3
Heart and circulatory	142	15	15	34	38	25	11
Respiratory	19	1	3	2	6	6	1
Alimentary	60	2	10	14	22	9	3
Genital organs	142	5	31	38	30	28	6
Urinary system	169	12	31	46	45	20	9
Musculoskeletal	508	42	98	141	114	87	15
Skin and integument	71	2	11	25	23	9	1
Chromosomal anomalies	138	7	16	17	23	45	25
Down syndrome	103	4	11	9	18	38	20
Endocrine and metabolic disorders	21	3	3	4	6	4	1
Congenital infections	0	0	0	0	0	0	0
Other congenital anomalies not elsewhere classified	110	8	24	31	27	14	3
Total live and stillbirths	**336,984**	**22,941**	**64,342**	**86,392**	**97,596**	**54,058**	**11,655**

1 See Introduction for details of areas not covered by a local register.
2 Totals include age not stated.

Table 8f   All babies notified - rates per 10,000 total births: age of mother by condition, 2005

Areas not covered by a register in England and Wales[1]

Condition	Age of mother						
	Total[2]	Under 20	20-24	25-29	30-34	35-39	40 and over
All babies notified	**44.3**	**48.4**	**42.1**	**44.4**	**37.8**	**45.7**	**63.5**
Babies with a mention of:							
Central nervous system anomalies	2.7	4.4	3.7	2.3	1.9	2.8	2.6
Anencephalus	0.3	0.0	0.3	0.0	0.4	0.4	0.9
All spina bifida	0.7	0.9	0.9	0.6	0.6	0.4	0.9
Eye	0.5	0.4	0.3	0.3	0.8	0.4	0.0
Cleft lip and palate	4.2	4.8	3.6	4.2	4.4	3.5	5.1
Other face, ear and neck	1.7	1.7	2.0	1.5	1.4	1.8	2.6
Heart and circulatory	4.2	6.5	2.3	3.9	3.9	4.6	9.4
Respiratory	0.6	0.4	0.5	0.2	0.6	1.1	0.9
Alimentary	1.8	0.9	1.6	1.6	2.3	1.7	2.6
Genital organs	4.2	2.2	4.8	4.4	3.1	5.2	5.1
Urinary system	5.0	5.2	4.8	5.3	4.6	3.7	7.7
Musculoskeletal	15.1	18.3	15.2	16.3	11.7	16.1	12.9
Skin and integument	2.1	0.9	1.7	2.9	2.4	1.7	0.9
Chromosomal anomalies	4.1	3.1	2.5	2.0	2.4	8.3	21.5
Down syndrome	3.1	1.7	1.7	1.0	1.8	7.0	17.2
Endocrine and metabolic disorders	0.6	1.3	0.5	0.5	0.6	0.7	0.9
Congenital infections	0.0	0.0	0.0	0.0	0.0	0.0	0.0
Other congenital anomalies not elsewhere classified	3.3	3.5	3.7	3.6	2.8	2.6	2.6

1 See Introduction for details of areas not covered by a local register.
2 Totals include age not stated.

Table 9 Strategic Health Authorities in England and Wales, which have shown an increase in the numbers of a particular anomaly compared with the average notification for that area and anomaly during a previous period, 2005

ONS Monitoring group[1]	Anomaly	Strategic Health Authority	Quarter
A	Central Nervous System	Thames Valley Avon, Gloucestershire and Wiltshire	June June
0A	Anencephalus	Norfolk, Suffolk and Cambridgeshire Thames Valley Shropshire and Staffordshire	June March March
0C	Congenital hydrocephalus	Avon, Gloucestershire and Wiltshire Dorset and Somerset	March December
0E	Encephalocele	Cheshire and Merseyside	June
0F	Other or unspecified anomalies of the central nervous system	Thames Valley	December
C	Alimentary System	North Central London Northumberland, Tyne & Wear Thames Valley Avon, Gloucestershire and Wiltshire South West Peninsula	June September June June September
2A	Cleft of palate only	North and East Yorkshire and Northern Lincolnshire Wales	September March, September
2D	Tracheo-oesophageal fistula/stenosis	North Central London Northumberland, Tyne & Wear	June December
2E	Atresia/stenosis of large intestine, rectum & anal canal	Avon, Gloucestershire and Wiltshire	September
D	Cardiovascular System	County Durham and Tees Valley Greater Manchester Thames Valley Avon, Gloucestershire and Wiltshire South West Peninsula Wales	March June June March, June, September, December September, December December
3A	Tetralogy of Fallot	County Durham and Tees Valley Thames Valley Avon, Gloucestershire and Wiltshire	March June June
3B	Ventricular septal defect	County Durham and Tees Valley Thames Valley Avon, Gloucestershire and Wiltshire South West Peninsula Dorset and Somerset	March September June, September, December September, December June
3C	Other septal defects	Avon, Gloucestershire and Wiltshire	March, December
3F	Anomalies of the umbilical artery	Avon, Gloucestershire and Wiltshire	March
3G	Other congenital cardiac, or great vessel anomalies	Northumberland, Tyne & Wear Avon, Gloucestershire and Wiltshire South West Peninsula Wales	March March, September September December
3H	Congenital anomalies of other vessels	Avon, Gloucestershire and Wiltshire	March
F	Urogenital System	North West London Avon, Gloucestershire and Wiltshire	June, September March, June, September, December
5A	Hypospadias/epispadias	Bedfordshire and Hertfordshire North West London Northumberland, Tyne & Wear Avon, Gloucestershire and Wiltshire South West Peninsula	September September, December September September, December June
5C	Anomalies of the female genitalia	Avon, Gloucestershire and Wiltshire	March
5E	Renal agenesis	Northumberland, Tyne & Wear	March, June

1. See Appendix D.

Table 9 2005 Series MB3 no.20

Table 9 - *continued* **England and Wales**

ONS Monitoring group[1]	Anomaly	Strategic Health Authority	Quarter
		County Durham and Tees Valley	September
		South West Peninsula	December
5H	Cystic kidney disease	Avon, Gloucestershire and Wiltshire	June, September
5J	Congenital obstructive defects of renal pelvis or anomalies of ureter	Greater Manchester	September
		Cheshire and Merseyside	December
		Avon, Gloucestershire and Wiltshire	March, June, September, December
		Leicestershire, Northamptonshire and Rutland	June, December
G	Limbs	Bedfordshire and Hertfordshire	September
		North West London	March, June, September, December
		Avon, Gloucestershire and Wiltshire	September
		South West Peninsula	September
6A	Polydactyly/syndactyly	North West London	March, September
		South West Peninsula	June
6C	Deformities of feet	Bedfordshire and Hertfordshire	June
		North West London	September
		Wales	March
6D	Dislocation of hip	Thames Valley	December
		Avon, Gloucestershire and Wiltshire	June, September, December
H	Other Musculoskeletal	Thames Valley	December
		Avon, Gloucestershire and Wiltshire	September, December
7B	Anomalies of the face, skull or neck	Avon, Gloucestershire and Wiltshire	December
		Dorset and Somerset	March
7F	Anomalies of the abdominal wall (hernias)	South West Peninsula	June
7H	Anomalies of lips, tongue and pharynx	Avon, Gloucestershire and Wiltshire	September, December
7K	Congenital diaphragmatic hernia	North and East Yorkshire and Northern Lincolnshire	June
		Dorset and Somerset	March
		South Yorkshire	March
7L	Gastroschisis	Thames Valley	September
7P	Other anomalies of face & neck	North West London	December
I	Skin and Integument	Norfolk, Suffolk and Cambridgeshire	September
9A	Congenital neoplasms (other than benign skin)	South West Peninsula	June
9B	Endocrine and metabolic disorders	Avon, Gloucestershire and Wiltshire	September
		Trent	March
9C	Trisomy 21 - Down syndrome	Thames Valley	March, June, September
		Wales	March
9D	Other chromosomal anomalies	Wales	September

1. See Appendix D.

Table 10 Number of babies notified to the National Congenital Anomaly System (NCAS)

Year of birth	Data previously published in Health Statistics Quarterly 29[1]	NCAS at 5th September 2006	Percentage change between data published in HSQ29 and data on NCAS at 5th September 2006[2]
1995	5,863	5,859	-0.1
1996	5,999	5,985	-0.2
1997	5,982	5,963	-0.3
1998	6,678	6,678	0.0
1999	7,765	7,986	2.8
2000	8,344	8,460	1.4
2001	7,791	7,864	0.9
2002	7,595	7,811	2.8
2003	7,262	8,116	11.8
2004	6,358	7,578	19.2
2005	..	6,938	..

Source: National Congenital Anomaly System

1 NCAS as at 1 September 2005. Health Statistics Quarterly 29, www.statistics.gov.uk/downloads/theme_health/HSQ29.pdf
2 Reductions in early years are due to the removal of duplicate records from the database.

Appendix A - List of conditions for exclusion

Reports of cases with the following anomalies are not to be transmitted to ONS unless occurring in combination with other anomalies:

Name of condition

Spina bifida occulta uncomplicated
Stenosis or stricture of lacrimal duct
Minor or unspecified anomaly of auricle
Minor or unspecified anomaly of nose
Minor or unspecified deformity of face
Minor anomaly of nipple, accessory or ectopic nipple
Congenital umbilical hernia, inguinal or para umbilical
Undescended testicle and unspecified ectopic testis
Congenital hydrocele or hydrocele of testis
Phimosis
Hypospadias when the meatus lies before the coronary sulcus
Abnormal palmar crease
Skin tag with surface less than 4 cm^2: skin tag, naevus, angioma, haemangioma, glomus tumour, lymphangioma, birthmark
Clicking hip
Clubfoot of postural original
Minor or unspecified anomalies of toe such as hallux valgus, hallux varus or "orteuil en marteau"
Functional or unspecified cardiac murmur
Absence or hypoplasia of umbilical artery, single umbilical artery

With acknowledgement to EUROCAT for permission to reproduce their exclusion list.

Appendix B - Example of congenital anomaly form (SD56)

CONGENITAL ANOMALIES — Form SD56

Identification number: ....
(The form of this number is not important, but should be decided locally to enable a particular case to be identified subsequently if required.)

NHS number of child: ☐☐☐☐☐☐☐☐☐☐

Health Authority of mother's usual residence: .... HA

Health Authority in which baby was born: → .... HA

Surname of child (first three characters only): → ☐☐☐

Forename of child (first three characters only): → ☐☐☐

Place of birth of child (please tick one box only): → Home [1] NHS Hospital [2] Other [3] Not known ☐
If 'Other', please specify ....

Date of birth of child: → (day) ☐☐ (month) ☐☐ (year) ☐☐☐☐

Sex of child (please tick one box only): → Male [1] Female [2] Indeterminate [3] Not known ☐

Whether live or still birth (please tick one box only): → Live [1] Born live, died within 7 days [2] Stillborn [3]

Whether single or multiple birth (please enter number): → Single ☐ If multiple, state number born ☐

Date of LMP: → (day) ☐☐ (month) ☐☐ (year) ☐☐☐☐

If LMP date not known, state estimated gestation: → ☐☐ weeks

Birthweight: → ☐☐☐☐ grammes

Home address of mother: ....

(Please include postcode if known) → Postcode ☐☐☐☐☐☐☐

Parents' occupation (just before or early in mother's pregnancy):

Mother: ....

Father: ....

Date of birth of mother: → (day) ☐☐ (month) ☐☐ (year) ☐☐☐☐

If date of birth not known, state age: → ☐☐ years

Number and outcome of previous pregnancies resulting in: → Live births ☐ Stillbirths ☐ Others* ☐

Status of informant (please tick one box only): → Doctor [1] Midwife [2] Other [3]
If 'Other', please specify ....

Congenital anomalies reported:

(A detailed written description of each congenital anomaly is needed so that ONS can code the anomalies to the 4-digit ICD classification. **It is important that no anomalies are omitted.**)

....
....
....
....
....
....
....

* 'Others' is defined as pregnancies that ended in other than a registrable live or stillbirth.

TA15/3 12/98

Appendix C - List of ICD10 codes included within anomaly groups

Anomaly Group	Congenital Anomaly description	ICD10 codes used for data on the National Congenital Anomaly System	ICD10 codes used in Table 1 and Appendix E (Abortions, Stillbirths and Neonatal deaths)
Central nervous system	All	G04.9, G12.0, G12.9, G40.9, G60.0, G62.9, G70.9, G71.1, G71.2, G80.9, G83.2, G93.0, G93.1, Q00-Q07	Q00-Q07
	Anencephalus	Q00	Q00
	All spina bifida	Q05	Q05
	Encephalocele	Q01	Q01
	Congenital hydrocephalus	Q03	Q03
Eye	All	H18.5, H50.0, H50.8, H54.0, H54.4, H55, Q10-Q15	Q10-Q15
	Anophthalmia	Q11.0-Q11.2	Q11.0-Q11.2
Cleft lip and palate	All	Q35-Q37	Q35-Q37
	Cleft of lip only	Q36	Q36
	Cleft of palate only	Q35	Q35
	Cleft of lip and palate	Q37	Q37
Other face, ear and neck	All	K07, Q16-Q18, R22.0, R22.1	Q16-Q18
Heart and circulatory	All	I45.6, I47.1, I49.1, M30.3, Q20-Q28	Q20-Q28
Respiratory	All	Q30-Q34	Q30-Q34
Alimentary	All	K74.0, K80.2, Q38-Q45, R14	Q38-Q45
	Tracheo-oesophageal fistula	Q39.1-Q39.3	Q39.1-Q39.3
	Oesophageal atresia	Q39.0	Q39.0
	Atresia/stenosis large intestine, rectum or anal canal	Q42	Q42
Genital organs	All	N47, N89.8, Q50-Q56	Q50-Q56
	Hypospadias	Q54	Q54
Urinary system	All	N13.9, N25.8, Q60-Q64	Q60-Q64
	Renal agenesis/dysgenesis	Q60	Q60
	Epispadias	Q64.0	Q64.0
Musculoskeletal	All	K40-K46, M21.2, M89.8, P94, Q65-Q79	Q65-Q79
	Dislocation of the hip	Q65.0-Q65.6	Q65.0-Q65.6
	Deformities of feet	Q66	Q66
	Polydactyly	Q69	Q69
	Syndactyly	Q70	Q70
	Limb reductions	Q71-Q73	Q71-Q73
	Diaphragmatic defects	Q79.0-Q79.1	Q79.0-Q79.1
	Exomphalos	Q79.2	Q79.2
	Gastroschisis	Q79.3	Q79.3
Skin and integument	All	D18.0, D22.3, D22.6, D22.7, D22.9, D23.6, D23.7, L53.9, L81.3, Q80-Q84	Q80-Q84
Chromosomal anomalies	All	Q90-Q99	Q90-Q99
	Down syndrome	Q90	Q90
Endocrine and metabolic disorders	All	D66, D67, D68.0, D68.2, D69.4, D81.9, D82.1, E03.0, E03.1, E07, E23-E25, E27-E30, E32, E34, E70-E80, E83-E85, E88, E90	
Congenital infections	All	A50.0, P29.4, P35, P37, P52.5	
Other anomalies not elsewhere classified	All	B27.0, C49.2, C69.2, C71.9, C74.9, D13.9, D14.3, D15.1, D16.6, D17.2, D17.9, D18.1, D36.1, D37.0, D41.0, D43.2, D47.1, D48.0, D48.7, D48.9, D55.0, D56.3, D57.1, D57.3, D58.0, F79, I42.4, K21.9, L05.9, P02.6, P10-P15, P20-P29, (excl P29.4), P36, P50, P61, P70-P78, P80-P83, P90-P93, P95, P96, Q85-Q89, R16.0, R16.2, R18, R19.0, R22.9	Q85-Q89

Appendix D - ONS Monitoring groups and ICD10 equivalent codes

		ICD10 Codes
Central Nervous System	A	
0A	Anencephalus	Q00.0-Q00.2
0B	Spina bifida	Q05.0-Q05.9
0C	Congenital hydrocephalus	Q03.0-Q03.9
0E	Encephalocele	Q01.0-Q01.9
0F	Other	G04.9, G12.0, G12.9, G40.9, G60.0, G62.9, G70.9, G71.1, G71.2, G80.9, G83.2, G93.0, G93.1, Q02, Q04, Q06, Q07
Eye and Ear	B	
1A	Cystic eyeball	Q11.0
1B	Congenital lens anomalies	Q12.0-Q12.9
1C	Other & unspecified eye anomalies	Q10, Q11.3, Q13-Q15, H18.5, H 50.0, H50.8, H54.0, H54.4, H55
1D	Ear, all	Q16, Q17
1E	Other anophthalmos	Q11.1-Q11.2
Alimentary System	C	
2A	Cleft of palate only	Q35
2B	Cleft of lip only	Q36
2C	Cleft palate with cleft lip	Q37
2D	Tracheo-oesophageal fistula/stenosis	Q39.0-Q39.3
2E	Atresia/stenosis of large intestine, rectum & anal canal	Q42.0-Q42.9
2F	Other or unspecified anomalies of alimentary system	K74.0, K80.2, Q39.4-Q39.9, Q40.0, Q40.2-Q40.9, Q41, Q43-Q45, R14
Cardiovascular System	D	
3A	Tetralogy of Fallot	Q21.3
3B	Ventricular septal defect	Q21.0
3C	Other septal defects	Q21.1-Q21.2, Q21.4-Q21.9
3E	Patent ductus arteriosus	Q25.0
3F	Anomalies of the umbilical artery	Q27.0
3G	Other congenital cardiac or great vessel anomalies	I45.6, I47.1, I49.1, M30.3, Q20, Q22-Q24, Q25.1-Q25.9, Q26
3H	Congenital anomalies of other vessels	Q27.1-Q27.9, Q28
Respiratory System	E	
4A	Congenital anomalies of the respiratory system	Q30-Q34
Urogenital System	F	
5A	Hypospadias/epispadias	Q54, Q64.0
5B	Other anomalies of the male genitalia	N47, Q53, Q55
5C	Anomalies of the female genitalia	N89.8, Q50-Q52
5D	Bladder exstrophy	Q64.1
5E	Renal agenesis	Q60
5F	Other or unspecified defects of urogenital system	N25.8, Q63, Q64.2-Q64.9
5G	Indeterminate sex	Q56
5H	Cystic kidney disease	Q61
5J	Congenital obstructive defects of renal pelvis or anomalies of ureter	N13.9, Q62
Limbs	G	
6A	Polydactyly/syndactyly	Q69, Q70
6B	Limb reductions	Q71-Q73
6C	Deformities of feet	Q66
6D	Dislocation of hip	Q65.0-Q65.6
6E	Other limb or limb girdles	M21.2, Q65.8, Q65.9, Q68.1-Q68.5, Q74
Other Musculoskeletal	H	
7A	Other anomalies of the diaphragm	Q79.1
7B	Anomalies of the face, skull or neck	Q67-Q68.0, Q75, R22.0
7C	Other musculoskeletal anomalies of the thorax and neck	Q76.8, Q76.9
7D	Osteodystrophy or chondrodystrophy	Q77, Q78
7E	Other or unspecified anomalies of the musculoskeletal system	M89.8, P94, Q68.8, Q76.0-Q76.7, Q79.5, Q79.9
7F	Anomalies of the abdominal wall (hernias)	K40-K46
7G	Exomphalos	Q79.2
7H	Anomalies of the lips, tongue and pharynx	Q18.4-Q18.7, Q38
7J	Congenital hiatus hernia	Q40.1
7K	Congenital diaphragmatic hernia	Q79.0
7L	Gastroschisis	Q79.3
7M	Prune belly syndrome	Q79.4
7N	Branchial cleft, auricular sinus	Q18.0-Q18.2
7P	Other anomalies of face & neck	K07, Q18.3, Q18.8, Q18.9, R22.1

Skin and Integument	**I**		
8C		Anomalies of the skin or integument	D18.0, D22.3, D22.6, D22.7, D22.9, D23.6, D23.7, L53.9, L81.3, Q80-Q84
Other Anomalies	**K**		
9A		Congenital neoplasms (other than benign skin)	C49.2, C69.2, C71.9, C74.9, D13.9, D14.3, D15.1, D16.6, D17.2, D17.9, D36.1, D37.0, D41.0, D43.2, D47.1, D48.0, D48.7, D48.9
9B		Endocrine and metabolic disorders	D66, D67, D68.0, D68.2, D69.4, D81.9, D82.1, E03.0, E03.1, E07, E23-E25, E27-E30, E32, E34, E70-E80, E83-E85, E88, E90
9C		Trisomy 21 - Down syndrome	Q90
9D		Other chromosomal anomalies	Q91-Q99
9E		Other and unspecified congenital anomalies	B27.0, D18.1, D55.0, D56.3, D57.1, D57.3, D58.0, F79, I42.4, K21.9, L05.9, P02.6, P10-P15, P20-P29 (excl P29.4), P36, P50, P61, P70-P78, P80-P83, P90-P93, P95, P96, Q85-Q89, R16.0, R16.2, R18, R19.0, R22.9
9H		Congenital infections	A50.0, P29.4, P35, P37, P52.5

Appendix E Summary table showing congenital anomaly statistics from three systems
National Congenital Anomaly System, Abortion Statistics, Mortality Statistics, 2004

England and Wales

Condition	Congenital anomaly notifications (NCAS)[1] Live birth	Congenital anomaly notifications (NCAS)[1] Stillbirth	Congenital anomaly notifications (NCAS)[1] Not known	Abortion notifications (under grounds E)[2]	Stillbirths - occurrences with a fetal mention[3] Main	Stillbirths - occurrences with a fetal mention[3] Other	Neonatal deaths- occurrences with a fetal mention[3] Main	Neonatal deaths- occurrences with a fetal mention[3] Other
All babies notified	**6,023**	**322**	**13**	**1,894**	**410**	**242**	**377**	**366**
Babies with a mention of:								
Central nervous system anomalies	277	82	3	443	81	37	58	43
Anencephalus	12	10	-	145	16	4	18	1
All spina bifida	58	17	3	90	15	4	8	8
Encephalocele	12	2	-	19	3	-	5	1
Congenital hydrocephalus	52	20	-	52	16	8	3	9
Eye	99	3	1	*	-	1	1	1
Anophthalmia	7	2	-	*	-	-	1	1
Cleft lip and palate	483	16	1	*	5	11	2	6
Cleft of only lip	123	3	-	*	1	4	-	1
Cleft of only palate	157	7	-	*	1	1	1	3
Cleft of lip and palate	203	6	1	*	3	6	1	2
Other face, ear and neck	151	7	1	*	-	1	-	1
Heart and circulatory	1,158	74	2	147	112	62	98	97
Respiratory	131	15	-	28	4	7	70	34
Alimentary	390	25	1	*	3	8	12	19
Tracheo-oesophageal fistula	48	2	-	*	-	-	-	4
Oesophageal atresia	13	2	-	*	-	-	1	2
Atresia/stenosis large intestine, rectum or anal canal	78	3	-	*	-	-	-	2
Genital organs	515	6	-	*	-	1	1	1
Hypospadias	410	1	-	*	-	-	-	-
Urinary system	694	29	2	69	29	15	25	47
Renal agenesis/dysgenesis	61	8	-	24	11	2	5	11
Epispadias	12	0	-	*	-	-	-	-
Musculoskeletal	1,855	69	2	124	41	38	49	43
Dislocation of hip	103	1	-	*	-	-	-	-
Deformities of feet	530	18	-	*	1	7	-	2
Polydactyly	307	4	-	*	-	-	-	-
Syndactyly	159	3	-	*	-	-	-	1
Limb reductions	187	8	1	*	-	1	-	1
Diaphragmatic defects	77	10	-	18	5	7	34	13
Exomphalos	50	7	-	11	3	1	2	1-
Gastroschisis	186	5	-	*	7	2	2	1
Skin and integument	213	5	2	*	-	-	3	1
Chromosomal anomalies	596	81	4	726	81	36	39	34
Down syndrome	420	34	2	419	17	15	2	16
Endocrine and metabolic disorders	150	3	-	*	-	-	-	-
Congenital infections	9	2	-	*	-	-	-	-
Other congenital anomalies not elsewhere classified	382	57	2	56	54	25	19	39

Source
1 National Congenital Anomaly System at 1st September 2005.
2 Department of Health. Abortion Statistics, England and Wales 2004, July 2005.
3 Office for National Statistics. Series DH3 no. 37, Mortality Statistics: Childhood, infant and perinatal, 2004, residents only.

* less than 10 cases